Anonymous

Fifth Annual Report of the Board of Trustees and Managers of the California Institution for the Education and Care of the Indigent Deaf and Dumb, and the Blind, to the Governor of the State of California, for the Year ending Dec. 31, 1864

Anonymous

Fifth Annual Report of the Board of Trustees and Managers of the California Institution for the Education and Care of the Indigent Deaf and Dumb, and the Blind, to the Governor of the State of California, for the Year ending Dec. 31, 1864

ISBN/EAN: 9783337184704

Printed in Europe, USA, Canada, Australia, Japan

Cover: Foto ©Andreas Hilbeck / pixelio.de

More available books at **www.hansebooks.com**

MEMORANDUM

ADDRESSED TO

THE HONOURABLE THE MINISTER

OF

RAILWAYS AND CANALS

BY THE

ENGINEER-IN-CHIEF

OF THE

CANADIAN PACIFIC RAILWAY

OTTAWA:
PRINTED BY MACLEAN, ROGER & Co., WELLINGTON STREET.
1880.

MEMORANDUM

ADDRESSED TO

THE HONOURABLE THE MINISTER

OF

RAILWAYS AND CANALS

BY THE

ENGINEER-IN-CHIEF

OF THE

CANADIAN PACIFIC RAILWAY

OTTAWA:

PRINTED BY MACLEAN, ROGER & Co., WELLINGTON STREET.

1880.

[*Printed by authority of the Honorable the Minister of Railways and Canals*, 10th April, 1880.]

MEMORANDUM

ADDRESSED TO

THE HONORABLE THE MINISTER OF RAILWAYS AND CANALS

BY THE

ENGINEER-IN-CHIEF

OF THE

CANADIAN PACIFIC RAILWAY.

CANADIAN PACIFIC RAILWAY.

OFFICE OF THE ENGINEER-IN-CHIEF,

Ottawa, 26th March, 1880.

Memorandum.

On the 3rd March, grave charges were made in the House of Commons, against the writer, as Chief Engineer of the Canadian Pacific Railway, which have since been published throughout the Dominion. These charges seriously affect his personal character and his professional reputation.

A member of the House of Commons has certainly the right to investigate the conduct of any public servant, if he deems it proper to do so. Equally the party assailed, if wrongly accused, may claim to be heard in his justification.

An Engineer is an executive officer of the Government, to whom the public interest is confided according to his rank and *status*. No charge can be more painful than that he has neglected his duties, or that he has failed honestly, and with ability, to consult the interests he has undertaken to protect.

1

It is obvious that, if called upon to vindicate his character from what he holds
bo an unjust accusation, the only course open to an Engineer, in the employ of t
Government, so long as he holds his position, is to address his remonstrance to t
Minister at the head of the Department.

Ho cannot with propriety avail himself of the colums of the newspapers or of
magazine, neither can he publish a pamphlet in his vindication. To the mind of t
writer it is still more objectionable to have recourse to a borrowed pen, and to g
published anonymously what he holds inexpedient to state above his signature.

The writer, therefore, respectfully asks leave to address the Minister on the su
ject of the charges made against him in Parliament.

They may be formulated:—That the writer has recom ended an ill-judged ar
unwaranted site for the bridge-crossing of Red River; that he was long absent i
England from his duties, during which time the railway work was unconsidered, ar
his responsibilities neglected; that the original estimates given for the work und
contract have been greatly exceeded; that he has caused needless expenditure
Cross Lake on an improper location, and, that he has permitted large sums of mone
to be carelessly wasted.

The writer has submitted, at length, the reasons which have led him to recor
mend the location of the Red River Bridge. They are set forth in his report to th
Government, of 8th December, 1879, to be laid before Parliament. Subsequer
enquiry having confirmed the facts he cannot change or modify his opinion
He respectfully submits that, if the question be examined and the facts and the circum
stances be fully weighed, it will be found that his view of the case will be sustaine
and his recommendation justified. It is known that the location recommended l
him is not looked upon with favour in quarters and localities adversely intereste
but his own convictions remain unchanged, and he holds it incumbent on him, in th
general interest of the public, to adhere to the selection he has submitted, and to a
that the considerations which dictated it be fully examined.

On this point of the censure directed against him, he begs leave respectfully t
refer to his report to the Government, and to ask for it impartial consideration.

3

He turns to the other issues which have been raised. The charge is unusually grave, that of having neglected his duty and allowed large sums of money to be squandered. An engineer is in no way answerable for the policy adopted by the Government in making contracts; but once a contract is entered into and placed in his hands, he is responsible to the Government, through the Minister of the Department, that it be honestly fulfilled. It is his duty to carry out and enforce its conditions, to see that the work is properly performed and full value given for the money paid. It is equally his duty to do justice to the contractor, as to the public; indeed, to act as a judge between parties whose views of right are not always identical. It is moreover, his duty to submit to the Minister any changes, in construction or otherwise, he may hold to be desirable, and, on obtaining the Minister's authority, to have them carried out.

Between 1863 and 1871, the writer was Chief Engineer of the Intercolonial Railway. From 1871 to 1876, he filled the position of Engineer-in-Chief of both the Intercolonial and Canadian Pacific Railways. In the latter year the Intercolonial was opened for traffic, and the writer ceased to act as Chief Engineer. At this date most of the difficulties connected with the Canadian Pacific location had been solved. Two sections, easy of construction, had been placed under contract; No. 13, the first section west of Fort William, Lake Superior, 33 miles; No 14, the first section east of Selkirk, Red River, 77 miles.

The writer's health had been much affected by his labours; his medical advisers counselled rest. He himself felt that abstinence from work was indispensable. He applied, accordingly, for twelve months' leave of absence. So much a matter of necessity did this rest appear to himself, that he had determined, should the leave of absence not be granted, to resign his position, a fact perfectly capable of being established.

Before leaving, it was arranged that the Senior Assistant, on the Pacific Railway staff, in the writer's absence, should assume his duties. Full confidence was felt in the ability, experience and reliability of that officer, and, on the writer's recommendation, the then Minister of the Department consented to the arrangement. That gentleman was placed in charge, and he entered on his duties with the title of Acting Chief Engineer.

1½

The writer left for England. At that time Sections 13 and 14 only were under construction. The work then performed was valued at—

Section No. 13 .... $127,353

do   14 102,140

Section No. 25 had been placed under contract as the writer was leaving, but no work had been executed. Six months afterwards the contract was signed for Section No. 15.

During his absence the writer was relieved from active direction of work, superintendence of details and all the incidental duties appertaining to his office. Matters, however, connected with the railway were frequently brought to his notice, and formed the subject of correspondence.

Twice he was re-called by the Government. His leave was thus temporarily set aside, and in consequence renewed and extended. Before six months had passed he was peremptorily summoned by the Minister to Ottawa. Leaving England in December, 1876, he remained in Canada until May following. In this period, independently of the other duties which engaged most of his time, the writer completed the voluminous Report of 1877, which he had commenced in England.

The leave of the writer was renewed, and he again left for England. He was again recalled, and so urgent was the summons that he started on a few days' notice. The consequence was that he was forced to neglect important private affairs, the arrangement of which necessitated his return to England.

In October, 1878, he returned to Canada and resumed his duties. The Acting Chief Engineer had, from July, 1876, held the position of principal executive officer of the Government to supervise the works under contract, to give directions to the engineering staff, to control the expenditure, and to issue proper certificates for work performed by the contractors.

From July, 1876, to October, 1878, no charge was taken by the writer of details of work under construction, beyond replying to the points submitted to him and receiving the reports forwarded from time to time. The latter in no way presaged the difficulties which now attract public attention.

On the return of the writer to his duties in the autumn of 1878, his attention was directed to the difference between the original quantities and the work returned as executed on Sections Nos. 14, 15 and 25.

Whatever the cause, it was plain that the original quantities had been greatly increased. No report of any such contingency had been made to him. The fact fell upon him as startling, from being unexpected, as it was alarming and unaccountable.

He had never supposed that a result of this character was possible. Had he been in the country his duty would have led him to take means to keep down the expenditure, to amend the line where change was advantageous and possible, and if through any cause the quantities of work executed showed a tendency to over-run the estimate, his attention would have been at once directed to the subject, as progress sections and the monthly returns conveyed the unwelcome information. No time would have been lost in endeavoring to ascertain the cause of the difficulty, and steps would have been taken to rectify it.

The original bills of quantities were made up without the exact data necessary for forming estimates with accuracy. They were prepared, from the best information, by engineers who had charge of each particular survey. As there was great pressure to have the work placed under contract, and definite quantities were indispensable, the results were, to a certain extent, assumed.

Much of the line passes through muskegs and marshes. The surveys were mostly made in winter when the ground was frozen. This circumstance doubtless, in some cases, deceived the surveyors as to its character, and led them to mistake marsh and muskeg for firm earth. One thing is certain, the quantities published before tenders were invited made no claim to exactness. Their *primâ facie* character establishes this fact beyond dispute. The amounts are almost invariably in round figures, such as 100,000 lineal feet or 1,000,000 cubic yards. At the same time, although estimated, or rather assumed, specially to admit of a comparison of tenders by having the different prices applied to them and the total amounts thus worked out, it was also supposed that if not approximately correct, they would at least not be greatly at variance with the actual results.

It was, therefore, incomprehensible to the writer that the actual quantities should in nearly every case be so much greater than those originally assumed and printed Making every allowance for imperfect data, misleading those who had made up the bills of quantities, for the frozen marshes having been considered to be solid ground and for other contingencies, in the writer's mind there was no satisfactory explanation for the extraordinary differences.

When the discrepancy came under the writer's notice, he at once gave it his serious attention, and the difficulty with all the circumstances connected with it was frequently and earnestly discussed with the Minister.

It was not possible for the writer to accept the returns of the work executed and the certificates which had been issued. Accordingly he declined to grant any certificates whatever, for what had been done during his absence, until the quantities were properly accounted for and irrefragably established as correct. He caused an investigation to be made into each case separately. He sent for those who had been engaged in the work to learn the course taken in carrying on operations, and the principle adopted in making measurements, and fully to satisfy himself as to the accuracy with which the quantities had been computed; but he failed to obtain any satisfactory information with regard to the excess of quantities.

A remeasurement of the work on each section was, therefore, recommended by him; a course approved by the Minister.

The value of the work certified as having been executed when the writer took the matter up, was as follows :—

On Section 13.—Gross amount certified			$331,978 00
" 14	"	....	583,742 00
" 15	"	....	1,151,975 57
" 25	"	....	1,180,800 00

In the winter of 1876-7, during the writer's stay in Canada, he was called upon as Senior officer, *pro forma* to put his name to certificates which had been prepared and laid before him. Their accuracy was not investigated by him, as he had the fullest confidence in the returns submitted. These are the only certificates for which the writer is in any way responsible up to the time he resumed his duties. According o the certificates which he finds in the office, work to the value of $2,539,181 has been executed in the interval, on the four sections in question.

In the case of Section 13, the writer was not called upon to take any action, as he work had been completed, the contract closed and the money paid before he eturned to Canada.

A remeasurement of Sections 14 and 25 has been made, but it does not verify nd substantiate the previous returns. In consequence, the writer has been unable to onfirm the certificates issued during his absence, for work reported as executed.

Section 15, and the circumstances connected with it, have formed the subject of special report. The facts have been laid before the Minister. Errors in the system f measurement and classification of work have been rectified. Explicit rules have een laid down for future guidance. A verification survey to check measurements as been commenced. The whole contract has been placed on a new basis under an Order in Council, dated 20th May, 1879, under which the work has since been carried n and payments made. No certificates have been issued by the writer since his eturn, except in accordance with its provisions.

These four sections only had been under construction when the writer reassumed is duties as Engineer-in-Chief; since then, seven additional sections, some of them ery heavy, have been placed under contract. He has taken every means to prevent a repetition of similar difficulties. The precautions adopted may, in part, be under-tood by reference to the letters of instructions to the Resident Engineers, one of which is appended.

From October, 1878, the whole time of the writer, and his best efforts, have been given to the discharge of his duty. From that date every point of detail, more or less, has come under his personal cognizance, and for the results he holds himself answerable.

This remark cannot, with justice, be applied to the period when he was on leave f absence, and he should not be identified with operations, over which he exercised no supervision, carried on during the time when, with the approval of the Govern-ment he was absent from the Dominion.

The question has been raised that the writer caused needless expenditure b an ill-judged location of the line on Section 15, in the neighborhood of Cross Lake

There are points between the terminus on Lake Superior and the Prairie Regic which govern the whole location. The geographical position of the Lake of th Woods on the International Boundary, defines Keewatin, at the outlet of the lake, be one of these points. Selkirk, in the writer's view, is clearly another. The pro lem was to connect these points by the shortest, best and cheapest route. With th exception of a limited area of prairie or thinly-wooded country near Selkirk, th whole distance is forest. A great extent of the surface is rocky, broken and rugge with many long, narrow lakes, some of which it is impossible to avoid. Cross Lak met some 36 miles west of Keewatin, is of this class.

The country here, and for a long distance, is exceedingly rough, and when th surveys commenced it was a wilderness, well nigh impenetrable. It was nece sary, however, to find a railway line through it, not simply a line over which train could be taken, whatever the cost of working them, but a railway which could b operated cheaply and which would admit of the conveyance of farm produce to th eastern markets at the lowest rates, a result only to be attained by limiting th gradients.

This view has governed the writer from the earliest inception of the undertakin In his published report of January, 1874, he set forth the paramount importance finding a location with the easiest possible gradients running easterly. He directe attention to it again in his report of 1877, and again in 1879.

Extracts from these reports are appended. This principle has been constant kept in prominence, and its importance has been generally admitted. It has be frequently brought forward during the last six years. The writer does not kno any instance of a public man having protested against it, or of any newspaper havir taken exception to it.

Although a great extent of the country between Lake Superior and the R River is very rugged, the general level over long distances is not diversified. The are no great elevations or depressions to control the location and enforce the intr duction of heavy gradients. Cross Lake is probably the only place on the whole 410 miles where any saving worthy consideration could have been effected by a departure from the principle of light gradients, which it was found possible to apply generally.

In the neighborhood of Cross Lake a number of lines were surveyed. Ultimately the choice was narrowed to two lines, connecting common points, east and west of Cross Lake, about six miles apart. No. 1 crossed the lake at a high level and gave the desired easy gradients, none of which exceeded a rise of 26 feet per mile, and the longest being for about one mile. No. 2 crossed the lake at another place, on a lower level, but it involved a continuous ascent of $2\frac{3}{4}$ miles, on sharp curves, with a rise of 44 feet per mile. The lake at the crossing of No. 1 is 600 feet wide; at that of No. 2 fully 900 feet; for five miles east of the lake the work is heavier on No. 2 than on No. 1, while at the lake, and for one mile west of it, the work is considerably the heaviest on No. 1. Although No. 2 would, upon the whole, cost less in the first place, No. 1 would undoubtedly, in the end, prove by far the most economical. After full consideration, Line No. 1 was selected, and it is on this line that construction is now being carried on.

The writer respectfully submits that the line which conforms with the policy of successive Ministers, and with the prevailing faith of the public mind, that on the railway between Manitoba and Lake Superior all gradients ascending eastward should be kept within the established limit, was the only one for selection.

It was according to this principle that the location was first made, and the writer respectfully submits that there is no act of his in connection with the Canadian Pacific Railway which should claim higher appreciation than his advocacy of the principle, and his constant efforts from first to last to secure to the country a line with the lightest possible gradients between Red River and Lake Superior.

It was six months after he left for England that the contract for Section 15 was signed. As a matter of course, before the heavy work at Cross Lake was commenced nothing should have been left undone to reduce its magnitude by revising and perfecting the location, and by every possible means. When the writer resumed his duties the work was in progress, and it was too late to make any change at this point, even if a change at an earlier stage had been desirable or possible.

The writer believes that he has established that the censures which have been directed against him are not warranted by the facts, and he respectfully submits :—

1. That he has not unwisely advised the Government with respect to the bridging of Red River.

2. That he has not absented himself from his duties without authority and without cause.

3. That he has not neglected his responsibilities, or subjected to injury the interests entrusted to him.

4. That he is in no way to blame for the original quantities being exceeded and the cost of the work increased on the sections in question.

5. That he has not caused needless expenditure at Cross Lake on an improper location.

6. That he has not allowed public money to be carelessly wasted; but that by every means in his power, he has endeavoured to control the expenditure on the work, and that he has earnestly endeavoured in all respects faithfully to discharge the duties of his position.

The writer trusts that the urgency of the circumstances which have called for this memorandum, will be held by the Minister of Railways and Canals sufficient justification for submitting in this form the facts which it sets forth.

SANDFORD FLEMING,
Engineer-in-Chief.

11

EXTRACTS FROM THE REPORTS OF THE ENGINEER-IN-CHIEF IN REFERENCE TO THE ADOPTION OF LIGHT GRADIENTS IN CONNECTION WITH THE QUESTION OF CHEAP TRANSPORTATION FROM THE PRAIRIE REGION TO LAKE SUPERIOR.

From the Report of January, 1874.

" One of the questions which will undoubtedly force itself on public attention when the Prairie Region begins to raise a surplus for exportation, will be the cheap transportation of products to the east. Looking to this view of the question, the importance of a location which will secure the lightest gradients in an easterly direction is manifest.

" The gradients and alignments of a railway have much to do with its capacity for business, and the cost of working it. It is well known that by attention to these features, in locating a line, it is quite possible, in some cases, to double the transporting capacity of a railway, and very largely reduce the cost of conveying freight over it.

" That portion of the Canadian Pacific Railway between Red River and the navigable waters of Lake Superior, is precisely one of those cases where the utmost attention should be paid to its engineering features. The reduction of the cost of transportation on this section to the lowest figure is a question which affects the future of the country, as upon it, to a large extent, depends the settlement of the western prairies.

" The more this portion of the railway can be made to convey cheaply the products of the soil to the navigation of the St. Lawrence, the more will the field be extended within which farming operations can be carried on with profit on the fertile plains.

" The information obtained suggests that it will be possible to secure maximum easterly ascending gradients between Manitoba and Lake Superior, within the limit of 26 feet to the mile, a maximum not half so great as that which obtains on the majority of the railways on the continent.

" I think the line should be located so as to have the best possible alignment, with no heavier gradients than the maximum referred to. But the importance of securing the benefits of an unbroken steam communication at the earliest moment are so great that I consider that it would be advisable, in the first instance, to construct the cheapest possible line. While adhering to the permanent location in the main, I would, with a view of accomplishing the desired object, recommend the construction of a cheap temporary line, avoiding for the present all costly permanent works that would retard its completion. In order to gain access to the country as speedily and cheaply as possible, it might indeed become necessary to overcome special difficulties by adopting temporarily, for short distances, deviations from the true location with heavy undulating gradients and sharp curvature. I have no reason, however, to think that this expedient would frequently be required. I am satisfied that for the greater part of the distance between Lake Superior and Manitoba, the permanent location may be substantially adhered to." (Page 32, 33.)

From the Report of February, 1877.

" It has been held from the first that the successful occupation of the Prairie Region and the extent to which it may become thickly populated will, in a great measure, be governed by the capability of the line to Lake Superior to carry cheaply the products of the soil. The success of the railway itself must be determined by the number of inhabitants which can be established in the country, and the degree of prosperity of the population will be influenced in no narrow limit by the character of the outlet for the products of their industry. The more, therefore, that the eastern section of the railway can be rendered available for cheap transportation, the more rapidly will the Prairie Region become populated and the more speedily will the line become self-sustaining.

"I have felt it my duty to regard these views as of paramount importance in the location of the line between the Prairie Region and Lake Superior. Accordingly every effort has been made to discover the shortest line, with the lightest possible gradients and easiest curvature, especially in the direction which heavy traffic will take, towards the Atlantic seaboard.

"On the sections placed under contract from Red River to Keewatin, 114 miles and from English River to Fort William, 113 miles, the maximum gradients are as follows :—

Ascending East.

				Per 100.	Per Mile.
"On tangents and 1½° curves, equal to 3,820 feet radius.				0·50	26·40 feet.
On 2°	do	2,865	do	0·45	23·76 do
On 3°	do	1,910	do	0·40	21·12 do
On 4°	do	1,433	do	0·35	18·48 do

Ascending West.

				Per 100.	Per Mile.
"On tangents and 1½° curves, equal to 3,820 feet radius.				1·00	52·80 feet.
On 2°	do	2,865	do	0·90	47·52 do
On 3°	do	1,910	do	0·80	42·24 do
On 4°	do	1,433	do	0·70	36·96 do

"On the remaining distance to be placed under contract, between Keewatin and English River, 183 miles, equally easy gradients have not been as yet, at every point, secured. At the few exceptional points, the location will however be revised and I have confident expectations that all the gradients will be reduced to the same standard, without materially increasing the cost of the works.

"Thus, there will be no impediment to the Pacific Railway carrying products from the heart of the continent to Lake Superior, at a lower rate per mile than those now obtaining on the leading railways already in operation." (Page 81, 82.)

*　　　*　　　*　　　*　　　*　　　*　　　*

"I have described the efforts that have been made to obtain a line, with the easiest possible gradients, from the Prairie Region to the navigable waters of the St Lawrence, and the paramount importance of this feature."

*　　　*　　　*　　　*　　　*　　　*　　　*

"Cheapness of transportation is thus to a certain extent assured—an important element in facilitating the prosperous settlement of the fertile territory in the interior." (Page 85, 86.)

From the Report of April, 1879.

"I have always attached great importance to the endeavor to secure the best location attainable for the railway. I have elsewhere described the efforts which have been made from the commencement of the survey to obtain a line favorable for cheap transportation."

*　　　*　　　*　　　*　　　*　　　*

"The whole of the railway between Fort William and Selkirk, in length 410 miles, is now under contract. It is with no little satisfaction that I am enabled to point to a table of the gradients which have been definitely established in this length. Under the contracts which have been entered into, these favorable gradients are to be carried into execution without having recourse to the temporary expedients which I thought necessary to suggest five years ago.

Summary of Gradients, Fort William to Selkirk.

Ascending Easterly.	Feet per Mile.	No. of Miles.	
Rise ·10 to ·20 per cent.................about	5 to 10	38·52	
do ·20 to ·30 do	10 to 16	17·11	
do ·30 to ·40 do	16 to 21	42·97	
do ·40 to ·50 do	21 to 26.4	80·11	178·71
Level......................................		108·06	108·06

Ascending Westerly.	Feet per Mile.	No. of Miles.	
Rise ·10 to ·20 per cent......... ....about	5 to 10	28·51	
do ·20 to ·30 do	10 to 16	10·91	
do ·30 to ·40 do	16 to 21	9·74	
do ·40 to ·50 do	21 to 26	12·83	
do ·50 to ·60 do	26 to 32	6·82	
do ·60 to ·70 do	32 to 37	10·65	
do ·70 to ·80 do	37 to 42	12·76	
do ·80 to 1·00 do	42 to 52·8	31·01	123·23
Total miles.............................		410·00	410·00

" In determining the gradients the rule has been laid down to equate them with the curvature, so that when sharp curves were called for by the physical features of the country, the inclinations of the line would in those cases be proportionately reduced.

" The practical effect of a sharp curve on a maximum gradient is to make the gradient heavier by reducing the effective power of a locomotive making the ascent, thus preventing the passage of full loaded trains over the line. The object has been, whatever the curvature, to secure a degree of inclination which in no case would exceed, on tangents, 26·4 feet per mile ascending easterly, or in the direction of heavy traffic. The contract profiles of the line over the 410 miles from Fort William to Selkirk establishes that this object has been substantially secured. Only at one point (eighteen miles out of Fort William) has the locating engineer neglected to enforce this rule. I greatly regret that such is the case, as it will involve an expenditure to remedy the defect greater than would have been called for in the first place, when the cost would have been comparatively trifling.

" With the exception referred to corrected, the portion of the Pacific Railway between Lake Superior and Manitoba is thus finally established with extremely favorable engineering features, and it may be claimed that when completed under existing contracts, it will be available for conveying the products of the soil from the Prairie Region to Lake Superior, at the cheapest possible rates.

As this portion of the Pacific Railway must, for a long time to come, form the great outlet of much of the Prairie Region, the favorable character for cheap transportation which has been secured for it cannot be over-rated. Indeed upon this important condition very largely depends the successful settlement of the vast fertile plains and the permanent advantage of the future settlers." (Page 18-21.)

MEMORANDUM OF INSTRUCTIONS TO MR. W. T. JENNINGS, RESIDENT ENGINEER IN CHARG OF SECTION 42, EXTENDING FROM EAGLE RIVER TO THE EASTERN END OF SECTION 15 NEAR RAT PORTAGE (KEEWATIN).

CANADIAN PACIFIC RAIWAY,
OFFICE OF THE ENGINEER-IN-CHIEF,
OTTAWA, 3rd June, 1879.

Memorandum.

The Hon the Minister has appointed Mr. Jennings to the charge of Contra No. 42, embracing all the works of construction required to complete the railw between Eagle River and the eastern end of Section 15, near Rat Portage.

1. A copy of the contract entered into with Messrs. Fraser, Manning & Co., h been furnished Mr. Jennings. He has also been supplied with copies of the pla and profiles and all the documents relating to the work to be executed.

2. The undersigned has verbally communicated to Mr. Jennings his views wi regard to the work and the manner it should be carried out. He has explained Mr. Jennings the points where changes may be made, and has indicated on the prof some alterations that suggest themselves in the grade line. These changes a suggested with the view of reducing and expediting the work, the Contractors bei limited to time.

3. Mr. Jennings is desired at the earliest possible period to direct his attenti to any possible change that may be made in the alignment whereby the work w be decreased without increasing the curvature or gradients.

The undersigned directs the attention of Mr. Jennings to the importance of, no case, exceeding the rates of gradients and curvatures, as follows :—

Ascending East.

On tangents and 1½° curves, gradients not to exceed ·50 per 100.
"   "   " 2°   "   "   "   " ·45 "   "
"   "   " 3°   "   "   "   " ·40 "   "
"   "   " 4°   "   "   "   " ·35 "   "

Ascending Westerly.

On tangents and 1½° curves, gradients not to exceed 1·00 per 100.
"   "   " 2°   "   "   "   " ·90 "   "
"   "   " 3°   "   "   "   " ·80 "   "
"   "   " 4°   "   "   "   " ·70 "   "

While insisting that in no case these gradients shall be exceeded, the Chi Engineer directs the earnest attention of Mr. Jennings to the very great importan of keeping down the cost of the work, and he trusts that wherever it be possib without lowering the character of the engineering features of the line, Mr. Jennin will studiously avoid incurring any expenditure beyond that absolutely required.

4. The undersigned recognizes the peculiar difficulties which will be met by t contractors in this section ; not the least serious being the inaccessibility of t country through which the line is to be constructed, and he foresees the great ir portance to them of having the rail track extended as far as possible easterly fro Rat Portage, the moment the rails are laid throughout Section 15. From 2 to miles east of Rat Portage, the profile shows some of the heaviest work on the whol section, after which for several miles the work is comparatively light.

Fortunately the difficult portion could easily be got over by adopting, temporarily, a steep grade, as indicated in the accompanying profile. Mr. Jennings is authorized to make this suggestion to the contractors, with the understanding that the undersigned will concur in its adoption, should the contractors desire it in their own interest. The line must, thereafter, be constructed with the permanent gradient before the completion of the contract, and the contractors will be paid for all now or hereafter executed, which forms any part of the permanent work. The cost of temporary track laying, and the small amount of excavation of parts A, B, C, D, etc., or any work of a merely temporary character, not necessary in the permanent works, will have to be borne by themselves.

5. For the guidance of Mr. Jennings, it may be mentioned that on some of the sections which have been under construction the contractors have found it convenient, with the modern explosives, to blast out rock cuttings considerably beyond the slope lines, as defined on the specifications. The Engineer-in-Chief directs that only the excavation within the slope lines be returned as rock. The material beyond the slope lines, if placed in embankments, may be returned and paid for as earth; but, if wasted it must not be returned as excavation under any class.

6. It may further be mentioned for the information of Mr. Jennings, that on some sections under construction, when muskegs prevail and the embankments have been formed from side borrowing pits and ditches, serious difficulties have arisen. The material so borrowed is reported to be, in many cases, vegetable matter of a spongy nature, holding much water, and when dry and compressed by a superincumbent weight, to have little solidity; it is consequently, unfit to be used in the formation of earth embankment. The undersigned accordingly disapproves of its use.

7. There is always more or less difficulty in forming embankments across muskegs or marshes. In some cases where a proper out-fall is available, so that ditches would have the effect of draining and consolidating the ground, it is advisable to form them parallel to the line of railway. But when the ditches, after being formed would simply remain full of stagnant water, their formation is of doubtful expediency, and under such circumstances, ditches are of little value. Indeed, in some special localities they may be a positive injury, and in all such cases it is advisable not to form them, but rather resort to a judicious use of the logging and brushing provided for under the contract.

This being done a thin covering of earth to form a foundation and bed for the ties may be added. Track may then be laid and thus allow material to be brought from any convenient distance by train. But if this expedient be resorted to, it will be necessary to bed the track sufficiently even and solid to prevent the rails from being bent or injured in any way.

8. These several points are brought to the attention of Mr. Jennings, but he will himself determine the best course to be pursued when he has specially examined each locality, and become acquainted with the depth of the muskeg, and all the circumstances. In arriving at a decision, Mr. Jennings will take into consideration the question of haul, for which a price is provided, and he will see that in no case the price of earth and haul together (when material is brought by train) shall exceed the price of ballast, as in such cases ballast would probably be the best and cheapest material with which to form the embankment.

9. There may be some exceptional case where it may not be impossible for the contractors to procure suitable material for the road bed and where it would be a very great advantage to them and expedite their operations, if they were permitted to use in part the spongy material found in Muskegs. This shall only be allowed sparingly, and in all cases when used, the solid contents of the spongy matter only is to be paid for. A log platform (clause 12) must invariably be laid on the surface before any of the muskeg material is deposited, and arrangements must be made to measure the solid cubic contents in the embankment after the water has had time to drain out of it. On these conditions as to measurement and payment and on these only, will the undersigned approve of the use in any form, of this peculiar material.

Mr. Jennings will be good enough to inform the contractors accordingly, and ob tain their written acceptance of these conditions, when the material is place in embankments. Wherever it be deemed expedient to allow the use o muskeg material, the whole must be covered over with good earth; in no cas should the coating of sand, clay or gravel be less than 12 inches under formation leve

(Sketch A.)

As a rule the surface of the muskeg should not be broken by ditches or borrow ing pits within 50 feet of the centre line.

10. When it becomes expedient to form the embankments by train, good-size poles, or small trees "spotted" on the side, to average say six inches thick, should invariably be laid longitudinally under the ties. These poles shoul break joint, and every means taken to render the track reasonably solid and secur to prevent injury to rails. See Sketch B.

(Sketch B.)

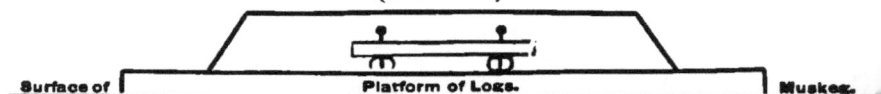

10½. The undersigned has given careful consideration to the question of rock bor rowing, referred to in the specification, and he has arrived at the conclusion that i will not be expedient to resort to the process of excavating rock for forming any portions of embankments, except so far as the embankments may be formed by material from "rock line cuttings."

The contractors will, accordingly, be relieved of this expensive and troublesome class of work referred to in Clause 98 of the specification.

11. Mr. Jennings is probably aware that on Section 15, where the railway is car ried across lakes and ponds, the material from rock line cuttings has been deposited in two parallel lines along the toe of the slopes. This was done subsequent to the date of the contract with a special purpose in view, but it involves a good deal o extra trouble and expense to the contractors, without corresponding advantages, and as the undersigned recognizes the peculiar difficulties, these contractors have to over come, and the importance in the public interest of assisting them in every legitimate way, and of avoiding unnecessary outlay, he does not insist upon the same plan of con struction being followed on this contract.

The contractors may be allowed to finish the embankments in the usual way, al lowing the material of whatever kind to find its proper natural slope, and in the case of the slopes being formed of soft material, in ponds or lakes, they will be protected by rip-rap, a few feet above and below water level. The rip-rap must be provided after the embankment has to some extent consolidated.

12. Attention should at once be given to the volume of all streams crossed by the railway; the necessity for the structures proposed to be erected, and their suffi ciency and character.

Mr. Jennings will report from time to time such improvements or suggestions in the mode of construction as may appear advisable.

13. The Engineer-in-Chief encloses printed general instructions 1 to 5 for the information of Mr. Jennings on the general guidance of the staff under him. These are in force as far as applicable. Special attention is directed to these general in structions.

The object in view is considered of great importance. Not the least important is to secure a complete historical record of the progress of the work under the contract, with details of every event noticed as it transpires. The purveyor branch, referred to in Instructions No. 2, is, however, abolished, and Mr. Jennings will himself be held responsible for procuring supplies and the proper account of all expenditure. It is the intention of the undersigned to apply for the authority of the Minister to make a money allowance in lieu of rations to members of the staff. In the meantime it is expedient to carry on the old system. Mr. Jennings will, however, be good enough and report if it will be practicable to change the system, say on 1st September next.

14. While the Engineer-in-Chief refers Mr. Jennings to the rules established by the Department, with respect to the making of payments, the keeping of accounts and the character of the vouchers required by the audit, he directs his attention to the exercise of proper economy in all matters of expenditure. Any food supplies obtained must be good and sufficient, and procured at reasonable prices.

15. While exercising prudence and forethought as to the wants of the staff, and the supply of good and sufficient provisions, all extravagance and waste and all unnecessary expense must be avoided.

16. The following staff has been selected to assist Mr. Jennings in carrying out these instructions:—

* * * * * * *

17. The Engineer-in-Chief requests that Mr. Jennings will issue a circular letter to the Division and Assistant Engineers, informing them that all orders or communications in writing made to the contractors, respecting the works, must pass through his hands and be signed by him alone, and Mr. Jennings will be good enough to report all orders so given and draw special attention to any matters of importance.

18. As far as can be foreseen, ample allowance has been made in the bill of works for every description of work required under the contract. Should it become expedient, as operations proceed, to execute any class of work for which no provision is made, Mr. Jennings' attention is directed to the 5th clause of the contract, which stipulates that no additional work shall be performed unless the price to be paid for the same shall have been previously fixed by the Minister in writing.

The recessity for any additional work must therefore be reported to the Engineer-in-Chief, and if approved, permission obtained as above for its performance.

19. Mr. Jennings will arrange that the monthly measurements shall be completed on or before the last day of each month, so that he may be able to make up and transmit the estimates to this office as early thereafter as practicable. All monthly estimates are to be signed by Mr. Jennings, and forwarded in triplicate.

20. In addition to the weekly progress reports a short report should accompany the monthly estimates, referring to any special features of the work done during the month, the progress being made, the length of grading done or track laid, etc.

21. The Engineer-in-Chief impresses upon Mr. Jennings the necessity of holding the division engineers, as well as their assistants, personally responsible for the accuracy of returns of work done. It will not always be practicable for the division engineers in person to examine the whole work every month, but they should personally go over a portion of their division each month ; the sub-division engineers sending their figures to them by telegraph or otherwise. The succeeding month the division engineers will be able to measure the remaining portion, and by this means they will test the accuracy of the whole, as the work goes on and become familiar with all details, with respect to which they are responsible.

22. Mr. Jennings is furnished with a copy of the contract and every plan, profile and document relating to the works under his charge. The undersigned looks to Mr. Jennings with confidence, believing that he will spare no efforts to have these instructions, and the works to which they refer, satisfactorily carried out, and that he will earnestly endeavour to have everything done with strict regard to economy.

SANDFORD FLEMING,
Engineer-in-Chief.

4